A NEURODIVERSE VIEW OF THE WORLD

My Poetry Anthology

DARREN W. STELLA

Illustrated by
JADE Z. STELLA

ACKNOWLEDGMENT

A special thanks to the following people and organizations

My parents, Q. Ching and Mark Stella
Tim Vogt and Starfire Council
Soma Mukhopadhyay
Helping Autism through Learning and Outreach (HALO)
Julie Tyahur
Katie Masotti

Without each of you, this poetry and illustration collection would not have been possible!

All rights reserved. This book (or any portion thereof) may not be reproduced or used in any manner without written permission except in the context of reviews.

Copyright © 2020 by Darren W. Stella
Illustrations copyright © 2020 by Jade Z. Stella

www.darrendives.org
Instagram: @darrendives_
Facebook: Darrendives
Email: darrenstella1@gmail.com

Editor: Leah Lederman

ISBN: 978-1-7359289-0-6

CONTENTS

Barriers	1
Overcoming	25
Enjoying	67
Creating	90

BARRIERS

NOBODY

There was a Nobody.

He was not existing.

His house was not there.

He never had a birthday.

.

He had no friends who said nothing to him

He could not say no

because he was not there.

He really could not be nowhere.

Nothing bothered him.

He was not in his mind.

Nobody tried to talk to Nobody.

SILENCE DEFINED ME

Everyone is defined by words.

Some words can be powerful and others mundane.

My word was silence.

This word holds two meanings.

Silence is getting everyone to listen.

Silence can also mean peace.

For me it meant no words, no knowledge or opinion.

My whole childhood I felt trapped in my head.

Vivid memories of someone telling me what to do.

Tons to say, tons to answer.

I laugh inside when people think I am stupid.

Now I can communicate.

Now I am on top of the world.

My name is Linus.

People may look at me

like I am a dork,

but I am a game changer.

I walk the line every day

for my country.

I see battle wounds

all around the field.

The blood is enough to

scare any skittish person away.

The wounds and limbs

laying around are enough

for nightmares.

This is my reality.

This is my world.

Survivors use

the best equipment.

Not all people are survivors.

Rifles are my lifeline.

I can hear the massive

cannon all day.

It is my nursery rhyme.

So, call me a dork

or a soldier.

One thing for sure is

I am proud of the brave

man I have become today.

Hatred is based on

how people look and religion.

I think

God is not

interested

in us.

It is we who

find ourselves

more important.

ONE THOUGHT

It is a struggle

to survive without

getting hurt.

I see a world where

everyone is trying

his or her best.

It is hard

to be good

all the time.

There is a limit to

everyone's patience,

and how much of it

do we have?

Life is so funny.

It does not tell us any reason

why we live and

most of us make up

our own reasons.

We grow and

we try to do something and

we continue to live.

Then we have no clue

what or how history will help us and

why we need algebra.

It is nothing to take seriously.

I don't take life personally.

Life is something like

air and food.

Technology revolutions

lead to leaps in our lives.

Merchants roll in

high profits.

It is flirting with our greed,

But inviting harm to nature.

I know you feel like the worst person in the world

I know you feel like vapor that can vanish anytime

I know you feel like a captured beetle having no place to go

These are absolutely appropriate

for someone to feel

But I want you to know that

you are special to me.

A SAD FACE

Once upon a time,

there was a little boy

from Cincinnati.

The boy was named Tony.

Tony worked hard every day,

but was never happy.

Tony was missing a companion.

A question mark

Tony asked himself,

what qualities he wanted

in a companion.

He wanted someone

who was loyal and

compassionate.

Someone who

was always there.

A shooting star

Tony had a bright idea

He would get a cat.

For he had no time

for romance

He was a successful

neuropsychologist.

JADE'S COLLEGE VISIT

Help me find the right meaning

to live with a happy heart for Jade.

I am sad that

I can't go with Dad to

see colleges I'd like to go to.

Road trips might be

happy and sad times.

It is about hard choices, to be

happy for Jade and

sad for me.

I am ok.

A man has some mental issues.

He tries to climb his neighbor's roof and

begins to meow.

It happens only during

the full moon nights.

It is a rare condition where people

believe themselves to be cats.

This is known as "Cat syndrome."

The neighbors are nice and helpful.

Whenever he meows,

they throw a mouse toward him.

Those nights he would

have plenty to eat.

The man would

forget everything in the morning.

One day someone video-taped him

running for mice.

He was shocked to see himself.

He started therapy.

He is making progress.

Now he tries to eat more and

hears more news to

keep himself distracted.

I think occupying other land is

a violation of human rights.

Every country or territory

must be respected.

I am so done with war.

Ever since I can remember

our country is fighting someone.

Every president promises to stop,

but continues it.

Jealousy makes truth distorted

The division of

our country

mars the flow

of rivers.

Floor produces a barrier for us not to fall below our basic principles.

A man was terrified of number thirteen.

Every thirteenth day of the month,

he tried to stay home.

He thought evil forces were

awake that day.

He was very scared of his boss

who was born on the thirteenth.

His boss had no idea that

his birthday was so trauma filled.

This man saw a psychologist.

But he freaked out,

when he learned that

the psychologist's office was

on the thirteenth floor.

The psychologist gave him tasks:

to learn thirteen times thirteen,

to eat thirteen candies,

to tie thirteen strings into knots.

This did not help.

The man ran away,

never to return.

TRAVEL

Ring of phone

Hey! What's up

The long drive home

Smell of fries

line of cars

You want large or small

Airplane smells

Empty seats

Long wait

There was a haunted hotel.

It was owned by someone from Switzerland.

People came there to experience the supernatural.

The guests noticed the running children

who would mysteriously appear at midnight

and play around the long passages

in between the rooms.

There would be midnight mystery,

when a beautiful woman in white would walk around

and through the walls.

These supernatural events would not hurt anyone,

so this hotel was always booked.

There was a movie producer who wanted to film this.

The night he stayed there, nothing showed up.

This movie producer did not give up.

For a week, he waited but nothing showed up.

The guests were getting very impatient.

They wanted their money back,

but the movie producer was stubborn.

He tried to resist.

Next night his equipment wouldn't work.

That made the hotel staff realized something.

They needed to have a rule in place.

All kinds of cameras and taping

were banned after midnight to

respect the wishes of the true residents of the hotel.

PUMPKIN AND GHOST

The forest was always changing seasons.

Half the time, can't barely see through the trees,

then it seems empty, needing more shelter.

The bad ghost had to leave the forest.

He made his way near a tree at the end of the forest.

He found a pumpkin at his feet.

Every day in the forest,

groups of people found a pumpkin to take home.

The bad ghost decided to hide himself in that pumpkin

in hopes to find a new shelter.

It worked out really well,

as he made his way to a new home.

Too bad for this family!

OVERCOMING

WHY THE CAMEL SMILED

Long ago, a camel was walking in the desert.

He was very tired.

Finally, he saw a man who promised to help him.

This man was a camel dealer.

He took advantage of the camel's trust

and sold him for a big profit.

The camel pretended to limp.

The new owner found the camel dealer

and asked for his money back.

The dealer had to take back the camel

because he limped and then set him free.

The camel smiled and walked back to the desert.

FIRST TIME VOTING

Here is another way my voice can be heard.

This actually makes me feel excited.

People who count the ballot will not know

I have Autism.

My vote is equal to everyone.

The ballot is mine.

I am one powerful voice.

USEFUL BOY

It was a windy Sunday

when people heard a loud sound

and came outside.

The tree in the park in front of their houses

had fallen on someone's car.

People tried to call 911 but

their phones wouldn't work.

The cables were damaged.

People lost power and

they tried to be patient.

There was a boy in the

neighborhood who had Asperger's.

He knew how to make energy

using sound by screaming.

He began to scream and

immediately power was restored.

Everyone encouraged the boy

to scream more.

He screamed throughout the night

till the power supply restored the power.

He was a very useful boy.

Someone witty

but with no friends;

Someone romantic

but bashful;

Someone victorious

but getting lost in crowds;

We respect both

competence and insecurity.

My personal value is hard work. Thomas Edison said it the best: "There is no substitute for hard work." I believe that hard work can increase independence and ease of life. I work hard on the computer that helps me communicate. Communication can connect me with the world. I will keep working hard for the rest of my life.

PEOPLE WHO HELPED ME

<u>Mom</u>

To the woman who will always fight for me:

You are persistent.

You are caring.

You are intelligent.

Thank you for never giving up on me.

<u>Dad</u>

To the man who always has my back:

You are strong.

You are dependable.

You are my safe haven.

Thank you for everything.

<u>Mrs. Tyahur</u>

To the teacher who is magnificent,

You are wise.

You are generous.

You are bold.

Thank you for your patience.

Karen T.

To the lady who makes me happy:

You are kind.

You are loud.

You are popular.

Thank you for talking to me.

IN UNPRECEDENTED TIMES

Spending time at home,

The crest of pandemic peaks,

Poetry fills the proud minds of poets.

Staying inside

gathers rotten twists.

The lustrous mother nature

unties massive mess.

Social inequality is

part of the reason for

the mass protests on

the streets.

We can get the authorities

to make laws to

protect people.

The private sector has

to make their own

decisions.

We act decisively,

We measure accurately,

We emerge challengingly,

We are dedicated to peace.

Riding a bike has

the magic to

gather wind that

blows in the body

of my being.

Riding a bike

gives me wings to fly.

I am a bird

that reaches new highs

Riding a bike

liberates my soul.

A little boat is like life.

It travels through calm

And rough seas,

going to a distant destination

FOUR SEASONS

Winter is plagued with

lack of life.

Spring gives us new life.

Summer is hot but

pays off the idea of life.

Fall leaves us watching

the end of life.

I am thankful for

the people who gave me courage;

the pleasures that uplift my life;

the places I like to go.

Changing equilibrium

causes chaos,

which

makes a

      P
        A
         T
           H
         W
       A
     Y

to new greatness

Learning

stimulates

the birth of

brilliant ideas.

The laughing

reactor stores

strong and healthy energy.

Jade is smart and kind,

not to mention hilarious.

She is always there for me.

She brings paper home

from school for me,

because I am too stubborn

and particular.

Why?

Autism gets the best of me.

I love how driven and

focused she is.

That makes her prime.

My sister will go far in her endeavors.

WHAT'S UP SENIOR YEAR

In crazy chaos,

Darren walks the cluttered halls,

Senior year I'm here.

Dear Mom and Dad,

I can't believe this time has come. Your little boy is growing up. You have always been the constant in my life. Without you, my parents, I wouldn't be here today. You are like superheroes. The time and effort you put in to make sure I have a good life is heroic. Not just a good life, a meaningful life. I know the cards you were dealt may not seem fair, but you are strong for me. I want to thank you for all the meetings. You listened and helped me along the right path. I know times won't always be easy, but I will try. Thank you for making me number one. Now let's graduate!

Love,

Darren

The time of sunset is the time to

retrospect about life.

There are reasons to be happy

and there are reasons to be sad.

Happiness and sorrow

must balance each other

like day and night.

I was carrying food and water for the victims.

They needed good doctors.

The place was leveled by the storm.

Many people were missing.

There I met a doctor, Dr. Marty.

His hospital was totally washed away.

He wanted some blankets and some stretchers.

We could not help him.

I felt helpless,

when I saw the condition of the sick.

Two patients needed oxygen.

I could only pray.

Then I met a little boy,

eating from the trash.

I found his parents and they thanked me.

Next I found some children,

playing with broken cables.

It was too dangerous.

I told them not to play there,

but children couldn't understand.

I called the company

and they immediately repaired the cables.

In a confrontation,
    I am bold to battle,
        I react to find a resolution
            I lead to be peaceful.

I am reacting

to this stinging

situation better

with a plan that

gives me routine

and rhythm.

A NEURODIVERSE VIEW OF THE WORLD

Caterpillars

sacrifice to

build cocoons

and turn into

butterflies;

Haute silk feels

Magnificent;

Wilderness

triumphs

in its beauty.

His determination was

blessed with dignity:

to love the resented,

to always welcome

righteousness,

not to mocking the meek wrongfully.

Power can

lead us to defeat.

Education makes

us confident.

We are respected

when we lead,

when we honor,

when we measure.

Investing in caring

in mankind

will make the world

a better place to live

We gain honor

by

calibrating

our behavior

to highest standards.

What I did

in story writing

is a great example

that

being different

means

good things.

Can't find a better feeling.

Sunglasses magnify the width

of shadow that keeps

UVA and UVB away.

We have the tools to shield

our body away from

harmful ingredients.

A NEURODIVERSE VIEW OF THE WORLD

When you let your mind go intense,

your blood wins.

Our body may lose battles,

but we need to win the war.

We can manage

our life

with skills,

reinventing weakness

into strength.

Start

small

when it is

really new

and really hard.

It happens

and it's okay

that it happens.

You can't always

have good ideas;

It's hard to always

love yourself.

Inside my mind

are hard thoughts

I try

to get rid of.

Coming out stronger

is success.

Doing

hard things

helps us

learn

from mistakes.

Nice things at home:

Rooms, work and library.

We can start

weaving our lives

with these ties.

A DIFFERENT WORLD, COLORFUL

See the world in different colors:

Danger in red water,

more sickness in the green sun;

sand in an orange fire.

Horizon fades down into blue darkness.

Blue clouds show signs of new life.

ENJOYING

An ordinary life is

a beautiful life.

A NEURODIVERSE VIEW OF THE WORLD

We can recite

melody to calm

our heart.

Love makes the glorious

heart race.

Stars rise or disappear.

For long half life like elemental radiation,

show care and radiance.

MOUNTAINS

Faraway there is a wind

Faraway are the hills

Faraway the sun is bright

Valleys full of morning light.

The hot air balloons

were flying slowly;

My heart was peaceful.

River and hope are like

peas in a pot.

Don't ask me how it is.

One can pair them and

be happy.

River collects rain.

If river did not collect rain,

It would be lost.

Hope collects future thoughts.

So, we need river and hope.

I would like to:

- hike in the park,
- read a book to survive,
- watch a video of world literature.

Fossils rock!

We hunted trilobites

by the creek.

We turned stones.

Next to shells there were three lobes.

Are they Arthropods?

BRING MORE JOY TO YOUR LIFE.

People are trying hard to

find anything they don't have.

Everyone is rushing to

get more of everything.

I think it is good to

slow down.

In my house, we celebrate the Chinese New Year. My mom is Chinese. My mom's relatives are from China. In China, it is a huge celebration. We do a mild celebration at my house. It started with a red envelope with money. This represents prosperity. My mom organizes nice and festive dinners. I don't like some of the food, but I love her for the tradition. I like the chicken and rice. Family time is big for Chinese New Year. I like this the most because it is not about tangible items. Chinese New Year brings me joy.

Chinese New Year 2020,

the year of the Rat.

In the East,

it symbolizes stupendous wealth.

In the West,

rat conjures up negativity.

But Mickey and the Rat

descent from same family tree.

It was sunny,

Day was funny,

Nose was runny,

I had money.

I was rich,

I met Mitch

who had a twitch,

We had a sandwich.

He had a friend,

He can depend,

His shirt needed a mend,

He asked me to lend.

I gave him a cent,

To pay his rent,

Off he went!

My poem can end.

At the Great Pumpkin Roll Ride,

I rode eight miles on the bike.

It was plenty hot and

the heat lasted.

When I rode,

the breeze blew on

my face and body.

It felt chilling and

refreshing.

My parents and I went to the Autism advocacy project concert. The performances were unreal. They made me feel like people with Autism matter. The musicians were really talented. They really made the audience capture the big picture. My favorite was the male singer. His voice was very powerful. It reminds me of Les Miserables. I would listen to him all eternity if I could. The Autism advocacy project is the start of something great.

24 HOURS IN CHICAGO

In the hotel, winter stays away.

In the museum, art on display

mesmerizes the visitors.

On the street, people rush

to their destination.

By the lakeshore, wind blows madly.

SELF-DRIVING CARS

Can make the roads faster

Can be more like a train

Can make us feel like famous people

going down the fast lane

Can be more fun.

A little chick sits in

the green grass

surrounded by

beautiful flowers.

He is covered with

feathers that are

yellow in color

and soft in fluff

His eyes are

light and bright

looking cute

and wise.

A long walk

in the neighborhood,

The sky was blue,

The sun was warm,

The wind was breezy,

Spring had arrived.

A NEURODIVERSE VIEW OF THE WORLD

We sing songs

to show emotion

to reach the time of the moment

to set the boundary of reality.

Moisture rises and falls.

The earth rotates hot and cold.

The cycle keeps us going.

A NEURODIVERSE VIEW OF THE WORLD

I like to stare at

the water in the bay,

imagining a place with

eternal comfort.

It recesses the

theater in my head.

Motivation to

try new skills

results in

success.

More time at home

means I can try more ideas

A NEURODIVERSE VIEW OF THE WORLD

It was a sunny morning,

I was funny and singing.

Clouds were small and white,

Sun was round and bright.

A cat was on a porch,

looking at my watch.

She was fat and yellow,

I was too slow.

There was no one there,

I did not have to care.

I like Sunday morning,

when I can spend time singing.

CREATING

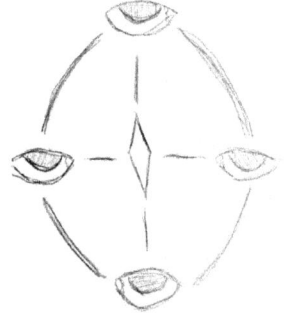

Right brain and left brain

seem to work together

some of the time.

Yet some of the time

we seem to have

two different minds.

The brain has magical power

to make sense of all of

our running thoughts.

Our mind also has to

tell our body what

motions to perform.

It seems to be a miracle and mystery

how the right and left brain

make up one powerful mind.

Science in the brain rules.

Controlling chemicals glue

our feelings to

dopamine and serotonin.

Ordinary people make

a good balance of them.

Me, always passionate.

Mist was fading

as the sun was higher in the sky.

The people saw

three strange lights in the sky.

They took photographs and

posted them on their Facebook pages.

A journalist was suspicious and

wanted to investigate.

He tried to analyze the photographs.

They did not look like plane

or helicopter lights.

The lights were triangularly placed.

This journalist was a science expert.

While everyone was excited about UFO,

he was studying the tricks

played by mist.

He discovered the mist

has a property that

can reflect city lights.

This phenomenon is called

Darren effect.

Problem was solved.

A Greek city was unearthed,

it was filled with strange temples.

Some of those temples showed

very strange drawings

maps and secret codes.

There was no resemblance with

any script from anywhere in the world.

A journalist was interested in

finding the meaning of the codes.

He had to measure the width of the doors

and the height of ceilings.

While investigating, he found a skull.

He was stunned.

This skull was three times

bigger than normal head.

The man was sure he had found

the city of giants.

He named the city Olympus.

A machine was found below the sea

somewhere in China.

It was ancient.

It was full of rust.

The scientists never knew

what it was for.

This machine had three needle-like structures

that went back and forth on a scale.

There was a leather-like strap

that had worn out.

Computer images made it

look functional.

The images were showing

a wrist monitor, a head monitor

and a chest monitor.

That was the turning point.

It was confirmed that

it was a medical device.

A NEURODIVERSE VIEW OF THE WORLD

Humor –

I went to England

in my time machine.

It was the twelfth century

and a fair was about to begin.

The people were crowding

around a big mud pie,

waiting for the chief

to break open the pie.

They had not seen me

or my modern clothes.

They were too busy

making noise.

But then the chief saw me

and they put me in chains.

Luckily my time machine was hidden.

The chief led the black birds out,

and asked me who I was.

I explained everything to him.

He wanted to time travel with me,

So I brought him to the current moment,

and took him to New York.

He wanted to get back home,

but my time machine

stopped working.

He had to stay here.

Today, he is in the White House.

Calm trees line the driveway,

as if they have something to say.

Busy on the grass are beaming lights,

filling dark sky so bright.

House up ahead leaves tries to escape,

From the magic of a musical tape,

the sounds of many alarming screams.

Most will run away from the scene,

except for one brave soul

who enters the house with one goal.

Much to surprise to see

the house inside was quiet and free.

Waiting beyond the door inside

was a bowl of treats

that could no longer hide.

Some lucky one should take it and run,

for Halloween is meant to be fun.

There are times

a thought turns

into a memory,

right like our thoughts

turn our life into purpose.

Some memories live

in our minds forever

to keep us present.

Others leave

without a thought

to remember.

Most of our life might be

forgotten if we didn't share

memories with others

Sometimes it is also nice

to allow yourself time

to be alone and create

your own memories.

She has long dark hair

She wears glasses

Her smile makes her

really wholesome.

Throughout American

history, immigrants'

hard work

contributed

to our society

a great deal.

If I were the king

of the universe,

I would make the

universe small

I would travel to

the farthest galaxy

I would plan

a galaxy party.

Family is the bedrock of our life.

Quarantine tests the light

Recognizing its toughness and flaws.

We strengthen the strength and

enrich interrelationships.

Passion appears

on your face,

when the caring heart is

lighting up.

Racism hurts the soul of

Ordinary people.

We do not only rant about

the unfairness, but also

mitigate its influence by

respecting everyone.

Research averages data collected into

Theories and models.

We ask more questions to

Validate and challenge them.

The process teaches us

lessons about the world.

Nature stimulates your senses with

wild essences.

Worst is to walk

without noticing

scenery,

sounds,

feel

and smell of

your surroundings.

I really want to be someone

people can visit,

when they need some interesting

new life ideas.

Maybe I will pass on some

good new ideas for little kids.

Pinnacle, like

most successes

recognizes that

we reinvent the

ordinary to get to the

extraordinary.

Buckyballs look like

a soccer ball.

They contain

only carbons,

connecting through

bonding and making

friendship.

A NEURODIVERSE VIEW OF THE WORLD

The wisdom of nature

masters the physics of

our environment.

We stay true to the rights

that tie the world

to nature.

LAKE ERIE

I wonder why it is so peaceful to stare.

I wonder why the rocks are so grained in the land.

I wonder why the lighthouse seems so abandoned.

I wonder why the sky looks so magical over the water.

I wonder why the tourists don't look at it the way I do.